Reflections

D0795283

"Your word is a lamp to my feet,

and a light to my path."

Psalm 119: 105

Janice Andrews

Janice Andrews

You are loved

DEDICATION

"You are loved"

dedicated to the memory of

Rachel Elizabeth Gilchrist

14 /12 /1990 - 15/ 09 /2013

a young woman

who loved the children of Laos

"Many women do noble things,

but you surpass them all."

Proverbs 31: 29

Janice Andrews

Contents

Janice Andrews

Contents

Janice Andrews

Acknowledgements

A sincere thank you to all who follow my Facebook blog "It's all about Jesus". Your feedback has given me the confidence to press on and collate my reflections in this book. Special thanks to Ruth Sullivan, book coach, encourager and dear friend. To my friend Pam for her experienced eye and careful proof reading. To my dear Mum, an inspirational lady who gives so generously of herself. Lastly but certainly not least to my Church family at Musselburgh Congregational. What a privilege it is to be your Minister and to share in the joys and sorrows of life with you and your families as we walk the great road of faith together, thank you.

"When the Chief Shepherd appears, you will receive the crown of glory which will never fade away."

1 Peter 5: 4

The Tapestry of life

Many threads are woven together to create the great tapestry of our lives. Golden threads of love and peace, silver threads of truth and justice, colourful threads of joy and happiness. However, woven among them are thick black threads of grief and brokenness, dark threads of hurt, betrayal and disappointment, and the underside of the tapestry is a tangled mess. Nothing makes any sense, it is only when the tapestry is turned over that we see how the threads work together to create something of incredible beauty. This illustration is most evident in the life of Corrie Ten Boom. Corrie was born into a Dutch family of devout Christians who were horrified at the treatment of Jews at the hands of the Nazis during WW2. At great risk to their own safety Corrie's family gave refuge to Jews in their home, however very soon a neighbour became suspicious and reported them to the authorities. The whole family was arrested and imprisoned and within ten days Corrie's Father was dead.

"No eye has seen, no ear has heard, and no human mind has conceived the things God has prepared for those who love Him."

1 Corinthians 2: 9

Corrie and her sister Bep were sent to a concentration camp where conditions were horrendous. As they lay together, starving, cold, and with nothing but filth, horror and despair around them, Bep whispered her plans for the future: "Corrie, people have suffered so much, and it is good that we have suffered with them because we understand what they've been through, when we get out of here we must do all that we can to help them to recover and to start a new life. What is most important is to reassure them about the love of Jesus, because nothing, not even the hell around us can take away the joy of knowing Him." Three days later Bep was dead. Corrie survived. She spent the rest of her life fulfilling Bep's plan, giving others hope by sharing the light of Christ. Corrie once said "Although the threads of my life have often seemed like a tangled mess, I know that on the other side of the embroidery there is a crown."

"Amazing love"
by Corrie ten Boom

"If we endure with Him, we shall reign with Him."

2 Timothy 2: 12

Endurance

"Endurance" was the name of Ernest Shackleton's ship. It was well named indeed for endurance would be needed for the voyage ahead. The great explorer was planning an expedition to the South Pole through the most inhospitable waters of Antarctica. Shackleton would need a committed crew to go with him and so he placed an advert in one of the London newspapers hoping to attract recruits. He was brutally honest, any men applying to go with him on this journey needed to be certain about what this would mean and what it may cost them. This was the advert he placed in the newspaper:

Men wanted for hazardous journey

small wages, bitterly cold

long months of complete darkness

Constant danger

safe return?   doubtful!

However, if successful, honour and recognition

SIR ERNEST SHACKLETON

"Fix your eyes upon Jesus, the pioneer
and perfecter of your faith."

Hebrews 12: 2

This was not a job for the faint hearted, embarking on this expedition with Shackleton would need total commitment. The greatest pioneer whom we could ever look to is Jesus, and like Shackleton, He too embarked on a recruitment drive. His earliest followers had been so excited to hear Him speak of a new Kingdom. They longed to be free from the dominion of Rome. The hated Herod Antipas was their King and the oppressive governor Pontius Pilate had jurisdiction over the affairs of Judea. Many began to wonder if it may be possible that Jesus of Nazareth would be the One to restore the Kingdom of Israel and take His place as the rightful King. However, what they had no conception of, was that His crown would be a crown of thorns and that His throne would be a cross between two criminals. With their limited understanding His followers could only think in terms of an earthly Kingdom with geographical boundaries, a Kingdom led by a strong and powerful political figure who would reign for a season. The Kingdom of God has no boundaries, Christ reigns over all the earth, and His reign is not bound by time or space, it

"Well done my good and faithful servant."

Matthew 25: 23.

is everlasting over all nations of the world. Jesus is looking for co-workers. He hopes that you won't cheer Him on from the side-lines but surrender your life completely to Him. He is calling you to step out onto untrodden paths, not knowing where they might lead, but having absolute faith in Him. Think of a guide taking inexperienced travellers on an extremely dangerous journey. He guarantees that he will bring them safely through, he will do it for nothing, he seeks no reward or recognition for himself, however, there is one condition, everyone in the party must yield in perfect obedience to his authority. Christ longs for us to turn to Him, our living, reigning, everlasting King with this same commitment. Are you ready for a wonderful adventure? The pathway is already prepared for you to take. It is time to step out, and you may do so with great confidence, for the one who fashioned you in your Mother's womb, who gave you breath and brought you into being is with you every step of the way and He will be there to meet you at the end of your journey.

"I will create roads in the desert, and streams in thirsty lands."

Isaiah 43: 19

God sees, He knows and He cares

Wherever your loved ones are in the world today
God is with them
Whatever they are going through
God knows about it
They may be far from your sight but
His eye, never leaves them

Our prayers are not always answered as we would hope, and in our toughest times, when we are desperate for help either for ourselves or for our family, this is so confusing and can lead to us feeling abandoned by God.   God will never abandon us.   It is often only with the benefit of hindsight that we are able to see God at work during the most difficult times in our lives.   As He works through these He teaches us so much.   It is only when we have walked a difficult road that we are equipped to get alongside others with compassion and some understanding of what they may be going through.   It is only when we have been sore wounded that we are equipped to tend the wounds of

"Even the hairs of your head are counted,

do not be afraid."

Matthew 10: 30

others.   God uses our trials to build us up in wisdom and knowledge of many things.   To develop ears that listen, hearts that truly care, and an attitude of gentleness for others.   God knows the deepest longings of our hearts.   He is making a new way forward.   He is the one who makes streams in the desert and new pathways in the wilderness. Trust Him with your lives and those of loved ones, He is working out His purposes.

"As the branch cannot bear fruit of itself unless it
abides in the vine, so neither can you unless you
abide in Me."

John 15: 4 – 5

God is the Master gardener who brings a harvest of fruit in our lives

A landowner rented out his land to a tenant farmer, and while on his yearly inspection he noticed a fig tree that hadn't borne any fruit, it looked dead. He said to the farmer, "I've been coming here every year for three years and I've yet to see any fruit on that tree, get rid of it, chop it down, it's only taking up room and using the nutrients of the soil." The Farmer asked for more time. He didn't want to lose the tree, he was hopeful that with patience, attention and care there was still a chance that the tree would bear fruit. He asked the landowner to allow him to nurture and tend the tree for one more year, to give it another opportunity to be fruitful. Jesus used this simple story to explain that this is what God is like with us. God is patient, we are His precious children and it is not His will that any of us should perish but have everlasting life, and so He waits patiently, another year, another season, another decade. However, we will only come to fruitfulness through Jesus, not by

"Be confident of this, He who began a good work in you will carry it on to completion."

Philippians 1: 6

our own efforts or by anything the world can give us. God is the Master gardener of our lives. He routs out the weeds that choke us, He confronts us with habits and behaviours that are fruitless and He challenges us to make changes that will move us closer to Him. His wisdom is given to us in His word which will never fail to bear fruit, God's word never returns to Him without accomplishing His purposes. His word is like a stream in the desert transforming barren ground into an oasis of new life. It doesn't matter if we feel that our branches are bare or if we haven't borne much fruit for a few years, God's strength is made perfect in weakness. He is waiting patiently. Come to Him today and ask for His Holy Spirit to dwell within you that you may receive from Him the beautiful fruits of the Spirit bringing blessings to you, and to others as He brings His purposes to pass.

Jesus tells the story of the fruitless fig-tree and the patient gardener in Luke 13: 6 – 8

"It is to one's glory to overlook an offence."

Proverbs 19: 11

Grace

"Chocolat" is a lovely story of a beautiful and enterprising young woman called Vianne who moves into a pretty little French village and opens a chocolatier in the heart of the village square. The locals are intrigued by her. She has a young daughter and yet there is no sign of a husband! In the late 1950's in a small remote village where nothing very exciting ever happened this fact alone leads to raised eyebrows. In her appearance Vianne was quite fascinating. Her style would not have been out of place in the most fashionable districts of Paris, but in this small village she stood out a mile. The local Mayor took an instant dislike to her. He assumed that as a single Mother she was promiscuous, and he found her flamboyant appearance coquettish and far too bold. He liked to control everything that happened in the village, but this was one young woman who would not be reined in by him or anyone else. He envisaged trouble ahead, her flamboyant appearance would be a distraction to the hard-working men of the village,

"By the grace of God, I am what I am."

1 Cor 15: 10

heaven forbid that she led any of them astray! And surely, she was a bad example to the local women who were so much more demure. The Mayor was a stalwart of the local Church and frowned upon anyone who was missing on a Sunday. It infuriated him that Vianne did not attend, although it did not altogether surprise him. Throughout recent weeks at Church services he had been reminding everyone that the season of Lent was nearly upon them and that they must be mindful to strictly observe this time of self-denial and reflection. He was absolutely furious to find out that on the very eve of the 40 days of Lent this woman was planning the grand opening of her shop. She was throwing open the doors of her sumptuous, decadent, chocolatier in an act of blatant defiance undermining his authority! For the next forty days the Mayor would be keeping his beady eye on the locals. There would be no indulging in chocolate, in fact he would warn them in no uncertain terms that even gazing in the window would be a sin! The Mayor would not be happy until he had driven Vianne out of his village. Each Sunday he spoke out

"My grace is sufficient for you,

My strength is made perfect in weakness."

2 Cor 12: 9

against her in Church warning the locals to avoid her, they must not be lured into her shop either by her products or by her charm.

Vianne is very aware of the Mayor's hostility and she has heard some of the ridiculous rumours he has spread about her, however throughout it all Vianne holds her head up high and conducts herself with integrity and honesty. She has nothing to hide and has no intention of explaining herself or her circumstances to anyone. Many of the locals begin to warm to her. She takes an interest in everyone, she is kind and helpful, friendly and approachable. This only infuriates the Mayor further until one night, fuelled by alcohol he decides to break into her shop and trash it, his plan is to drive her out of the village for good. In his drunken state he wrecks the shop but not before he has eaten a lot of chocolate. He ends up very sick and falls asleep, lying in an undignified heap in the shop window where he will be open to the ridicule of the whole village in the morning. Fortunately for him, the person who finds him in this

"God opposes the proud but shows favour to the humble."

James 4: 6

debauched state is Vianne.   Vianne realises the terrible shame the Mayor will bring upon himself if people see him in this state of debauchery and how he will completely lose his reputation if they ever find out that he has acted with such malice.   Vianne acts quickly, she puts shutters over the windows and a closed sign on the door to protect the Mayor from prying eyes.   She cleans his clothes and makes him a coffee, and while he gradually sobers up she turns to the task of clearing up the mess in her shop and putting things back in order.   The Mayor is so ashamed he cannot look Vianne in the eye.   He doesn't deserve such grace, he will never be able to thank her for what she's done for him, and he will try somehow to show her how regretful he is for how he has treated her in the past.   The villagers never did find out what happened that night, all they know is that the Mayor was a changed man. He became a much nicer person, more   tolerant   of   others,   kinder   and   more approachable. The strangest thing of all which none of the villagers could fathom was that he seemed to have a complete change of heart regarding the

"Get rid of all bitterness, passion, and anger. No more shouting or insults, no more hateful feelings of any sort. Instead, be kind and tender-hearted to one another, and forgive one another, as God has forgiven you through Christ."

Ephesians 4:31-32

beautiful young woman who ran the chocolatier, in fact he had become quite rotund as he was such a regular customer in her shop! The Mayor had been so blinded by narrow minded prejudices and so self-righteous, very proud and protective of his position in the village that the lovely qualities of love, kindness and goodness in Vianne's character had escaped him. What turned the situation on its head was Vianne's grace. Grace withholds from us the punishment which we deserve and gives to us the forgiveness which we do not.

In recent years the most powerful example of grace was In November 1990 when Nelson Mandela was released from prison. White South Africans held their collective breath, the wellbeing of their future depended greatly on the words that would come from this man's mouth. After 27 years in prison, Nelson Mandela, without a trace of bitterness, said "let bygones be bygones, let us focus on the shared future

"Father forgive them, for they know

not what they do."

Luke 23: 32

that we have together," and with these few gracious words the nation moved forward in unity.   Thank God for men and women who have the substance of character possessed by Nelson Mandela, sadly they are few in number. He gave hope to a nation through his attitude of humility and grace, setting a great example of what is possible when we love one another. Grace builds bridges, it looks forward with hope.   Grace brings healing to relationships, binds families together and builds stronger communities.

We will never be called upon to show more grace than that which has been shown to us. Jesus stepped down from His everlasting Kingdom of light into this dark world where He was falsely accused, brutalised, mocked, humiliated and crucified and yet on the point of death His prayer for us was "Father forgive them for they know not what they do," that's grace!   Let us respond by stepping out into our shared future together, demonstrating love, patience and tolerance, overlooking the flaws that we all have and embracing all that unites us.

"You are precious in my sight, and I love you."

Isaiah 43: 4

You are a child of God

A wee boy was walking in the forest one day with his Dad hand in hand.   As they moved thicker into the woods Dad asked the wee boy "are you lost Son?" The wee boy replied "no Dad I'm fine."   After another 10 minutes or so walking, Dad asked the same question "are you lost Son?"   And once again the wee said "no Dad, I'm fine."   For a third time, a little while later, the Dad asked this same question, the wee boy with some frustration in his voice turned to his Dad and said, "Dad, I'm not lost, I don't know where I am, but I'm not lost 'cause I'm with you!"   With our hand in our Father's hand we are never lost.

Simba, the little cub in the movie "The Lion King" felt hopelessly lost.   His Dad, Musaffa had been a very wise and respected King.   He loved Simba and had so carefully taught him everything that he should know to equip him to become the Lion King and to take his place in the great circle of life.   However, when Musaffa tragically died, Simba was deceived

"I will be a father to you, and you shall be

sons and daughters to Me."

2 Corinthians 6: 19

into believing that he was responsible. He was so ashamed. He ends up lost and alone, far from home, feeling unable to return to the pride, unworthy to take his place as the Lion King. One night as he stares into a pond he sees his Father's reflection and he hears his Father's voice calling to him "Simba, Simba, you seem to have forgotten me." Simba cried out, "no way Father I could never forget you." Musaffa replied "You are not living your life in light of who you are. You are not facing up to the responsibilities of being my son. You have forgotten who you are and therefore you have forgotten me." Suddenly Simba saw himself in light of who he was in relation to his Father. How could he have lost sight of the fact that he was the son of the King? He must honour his Father by living accordingly. Never again would he doubt his strength and abilities, he was the son of the King! God calls us to remember who we are, and whose we are, for we are His, we are children of the King, and when we see ourselves in light of this truth it is life changing and our confidence soars as it is not self confidence but confidence in God.

"Yesterday is gone, tomorrow has not yet come, we have only today, let us begin."

Mother Theresa

All too often we are like little Simba, crushed by our mistakes, guilt ridden by things we cannot change, dwelling on failures and losing sight of our unique and wonderful gifts.   This negative way of seeing ourselves prevents us from embracing life.   Stop looking inwardly and start looking upwardly! Remember who you are.   There are only two days when nothing is possible, yesterday and tomorrow. Today is a gift, embrace it.   In God's eyes you are precious, He calls you to take your place in the great circle of life.   Look to Him to be defined.   You are His child, live in accordance with this truth.   With God there is always a new beginning.   Look to Him for encouragement, for guidance and for wisdom.

He will never fail you.

He will always love you.

You are His.

"Wisdom is more precious than rubies, and nothing you desire can compare with her."

Proverbs: 8: 11

Wisdom's call

The book of Proverbs shows us two contrasting paths that we are free to follow; the path of folly and the path of wisdom.   The story begins in chapter 7 by introducing us to folly.   A young man is walking aimlessly along a street, it's not the best of areas, he is on his own and it's late at night, already we are getting the sense that he is not entirely safe.   He turns the corner and is approached by a prostitute.   She seduces him with smooth talk, saying to him, "let's enjoy ourselves until morning, my husband is not at home, he has gone on a long journey, he took his purse filled it with money and will not be home until the full moon."   The young man takes little persuasion to accept her offer.   As he disappears into the night the writer of Proverbs compares him to a young deer being caught in a noose, or to a bird being caught in a snare.   The fellow is out of his depth, he is likely to regret his decision not only in the morning but for a long time to come, for there will be consequences which he will have to face.   His actions

"How much better it is to acquire

wisdom than gold."

Proverbs 16: 16

are likely to bring trouble to his door, and when trouble comes to our door, it rarely affects solely the individual concerned, more often than not it ripples through the whole family causing worry and tension for everyone.

In the eyes of the world when someone gets themselves into trouble, there is a tendency to say "they've made their bed, they'll have to lie in it." Often, years later the incident is still being brought up in conversation, casting aspersions upon the character of those involved. This is not the response of our God. When we come to God truly regretting our bad choices and asking for forgiveness, He offers us a new beginning. With God there is always a clean slate. He does not keep an account of past sins, once they are confessed before Him, they are forgotten. Wherever you encounter God's wisdom you will also encounter His grace and His love, for they are inseparable. Chapter 8 introduces us to a very different character who we shall refer to as Lady Wisdom. In contrast to the adulteress who beckons

"Fools give full vent to their rage,

but the wise bring calm in the end."

Proverbs 29: 11

fools in the darkness of the night to choose the path of destruction, Lady Wisdom stands in broad daylight in the middle of the town square where all can see and hear her. She goes out to the highways and the byways and to every junction on the roads to speak to all who will listen to her. She offers lessons in life that are more valuable than gold or silver. She uses her words to bring truth. Wisdom is so important to God that He gave it pre-eminence at the beginning of creation. All that God does is wise for He is wise. Those who follow His wisdom are living their lives in accordance with His will. God's perfect wisdom is found in the person of Christ Jesus our Lord. When we ask Jesus to come and make His dwelling within us He opens our eyes and our ears, our hearts and our minds to the things of God. These are the real and lasting treasures of life which the world cannot give us. God's wisdom is tempered with love and grace, it is not self-seeking, it is always self-giving. God's wisdom builds us up in integrity and sincerity and in love for one another. God calls you to live your life in alignment with His perfect will.

"The Lord is my rock."

Psalm 18: 2

Christ is our Rock

There are times in our lives when we just cannot see the way ahead. It is as if our minds are fog bound. In our deepest trials we can feel paralysed, unable to think or to take a step forward, as if we are caught in a web of fear and confusion. It is in moments like these that Christ draws ever closer to us and calls us to look to Him and to Him alone. He is greater than your greatest problem and stronger than the pressure you are under. You may feel that you are walking on sinking sand, but He is solid rock. Many things will fail you in life but Christ? Never!

Christ is there.
He has always been there.
He will always be there.
He is sufficient.

When all you have is Christ, you have all you need. He will give you a strength beyond yourself. He is the quiet place in the storms of life, your safe harbour. In Him you stand on solid ground. May His loving arms keep you in His gentle embrace.

"Come and follow me."

Mark 1: 17

What are you tied to?

Two young lads were walking through a farm one day when they came across a well. They looked into it but it was so deep that they couldn't see the bottom. They wanted to try to find out just how deep it was so they looked around for something to throw into the well. There was a large, heavy cast iron radiator lying nearby, so together they managed to haul it up and throw it over the side. They were listening for it to hit the water when suddenly they noticed a goat charging straight towards them. They just managed to get out of its way, scattering to avoid it, and then to their horror they watched helplessly as the goat jumped head first into the well. A few minutes later the farmer came along, "have you seen my goat he asked?" "Have we seen your goat, we surely have, it nearly killed us, it came straight at us, you should have that animal tied up!" "That's strange," said the farmer, "I'm sure I tied it up this morning to an old cast iron radiator that was lying around!" The moral of the story is that we will follow whatever we are tied to. Many things we tie ourselves to are fickle

"I am the way, the truth and the life."

John 14: 6

and a waste of valuable time. Many may be frivolous but they are harmless, however there are others that are detrimental to our wellbeing and can lead to addiction or damaging relationships bringing no end of grief into our home and family life. Being tied to Christ is safe. He will never hurt you, He will always be faithful to you. He is your trusted friend and confidante, He will always encourage and support you. If only you realised how sufficient He is. Often we pray the wrong prayer, we ask God to provide the answers to our problems, instead of realising and trusting that He **IS** the answer! We look past Him, we look beyond Him, rather than to Him. Christ is sufficient. He is all you need. Tie yourself to Him, ask Him to dwell in you and you in Him. He will fill you with peace and lead you in paths that are always good and true.

"I am going to prepare a place for you and I shall come back and take you to be with me, so that you also may be where I am."

John 14: 3

Our King has prepared a place for us

In the film, "Coming to America", Eddie Murphy played the part of an African Prince. He decided to travel to America to find himself a wife. He wanted to be loved for the man he was, and so he left the grandeur of his Kingdom behind him and lived in America like an ordinary citizen until he met the woman with whom he wished to share his life. She fell in love with him, not realising that one day she would be a Queen and return with Him to reign with Him in His Kingdom. Those who love Christ are described as His bride and one day He will take us home to reign with Him. When He left this earth, He promised his Disciples that He was going to prepare a place for them, so that they too could be where He is. Followers of Christ have dual citizenship, we live in this world but ultimately, we shall go home to be with our King and we shall receive the very rich inheritance He has for us. This promised hope of the joy that awaits us at the end of our earthly lives changes our perspective on all that life throws at us.

"Everlasting joy will crown their heads, gladness
and joy will overtake them, and sorrow and sighing
will flee away."

Isaiah 35: 10b

Our greatest trials are light and short lived when compared to the glory that is before us. We are given a glimpse of the beauty and peace of God's Kingdom in the book of Revelation: "Never again will they hunger, never again will they thirst, the sun will not beat upon them nor any scorching heat for the Lamb at the centre of the throne will be their shepherd. He will lead them to springs of living water and God will wipe away every tear from their eyes."

Rev 7: 16 – 17

Jesus, our King of love, stepped down from His heavenly realm, lived like an ordinary man, making Himself nothing, dying on a cross, paying our debt in full and reconciling us to God giving us the promise of eternal and abundant life. Wow, what a King!

Christ your Shepherd King will lead you to springs of living water, God will wipe away every tear from your eyes and you shall reign with Him forevermore.

"Love is patient, love is kind,
it does not envy, it does not boast,
it is not proud."

1 Corinthians 13

God is love

God is love, and out of dust He created humanity with the capacity for love. We are a people of consciousness and imagination with the ability to know our creator. We are His treasured possession, we cannot begin to imagine how deeply we are loved. The world is crying out for love, but people are looking in all the wrong places. We are living in a generation that is surely more connected than any other in history, with the invention of the internet and countless social networking sites. How is it then that with all these opportunities of connecting with others more and more people are living in isolation? Statistics show that loneliness is a major problem in the most developed nations of the world. The older generation boast about how they used to know everyone in the community. How life has changed! It is now possible to live in a virtual reality without actually coming into contact with another human being! We sometimes despair over the direction in which the world is moving, leading us to ask "Why

"Love always protects, always trusts, always hopes
and always perseveres."

1 Corinthians 13

would God create the world only for things to go so badly wrong?" Well, let us examine this question in the context of a young couple planning to have a family. The young couple are motivated solely by love. They don't sit down and analyse all that could go wrong. Love doesn't foresee breakdown or trouble, love loves, love trusts, love hopes and love perseveres. These are the beautiful qualities of human love but they are only a pale reflection of the abundant love of God. When we lose our way, then if God's nature was not love He could respond by condemning us, but there is no condemnation in love. Love finds a way, and that way is Christ.

Christ is the bridge between time and eternity. Follow Him, He is the path that leads us home to our Creator God. God created us for eternity, He created us for peace and joy. He gives us His promise that one day He will right all wrongs, and all who love Him will inherit all the blessings that He has stored up since before the beginning of time.

"No eye has seen, no ear has heard, no human mind has conceived the things God has prepared for those who love Him."

1 Corinthians 2: 9

Fix your eyes upon the eternal promises of God recorded in the book of Revelation: "Look, the dwelling place of God is with His people. He will wipe away every tear from their eyes, there will be no more death, or mourning or crying or pain, for the old order of things has passed away."

Rev: 21: 3 - 4

This is the wonderful hope of the Christian faith. God did not leave us in our sin. Love pursues what is lost and love forgives. We cannot begin to imagine how deeply we are loved, thanks be to our God whose very nature is love.

"Do all the good you can, by all the means you can, in all the ways you can, in all the places you can, to all the people you can, for as long as you can."

John Wesley

Show goodness to others

A few years ago BBC Scotland made a BAFTA-award winning documentary series called "The Scheme". It followed the lives of six families from Onthank and Knockinlaw in Kilmarnock. These estates are lovely, full of good people, the neighbourhood is particularly close-knit, everyone knows everyone else and they are all there for one another. However, some of the individuals and families that the documentary focussed on lived particularly chaotic lifestyles. One young man was recently out of jail. He had never worked and didn't expect to find any work. He was involved in the drug scene and may have been written off by many as "a no-hoper". But there was a moment in the filming which was so powerful, viewers were stopped in their tracks, it happened when this chap turned to the interviewer, and as if he was groping to find some sort of explanation for everything that had gone wrong in his life, he said, "I've never known any goodness in my life."

"Do ordinary things with extraordinary love."

Mother Theresa

It was a profound and heart-breaking statement. This young man who was in his middle 30's had never experienced goodness, he had never received it, and therefore didn't know how to live it out.

God could choose any number of ways to engage in this world, but He has chosen to do so through humanity. We are called to be a manifestation of His goodness. To be His ears, listening to those in distress, to be His hands reaching out with love and extending the offer of practical help, to be His feet willing to go into the dark corners of the world where we find the homeless, the broken, the addict, the destitute. God calls us to reveal His goodness to the world. We may be rejected but we must accept this, for our faithful service is never about us. It was Mother Theresa who said "the good you do today, people will often forget tomorrow; do good anyway." God has called us to be bearers of His light that young men, like this young man in "the scheme" may know goodness, it may not change their lives but they will

"As the Father sent me I am sending you."

John 20: 21

always remember it. They will look back on all the chaos and dirt and grime of their lives and in the midst of all the dark memories there will be a light, a good memory, a time when someone cared, when someone reached out to them with the offer of help. Someone got down on their knees in the middle of the mess with them and tried to lift them up. Give the world the best you have, and it may never be enough, but give it anyway.

"Blessed are the pure in heart,

for they shall see God."

Matthew 5: 8

Blessed are the pure in heart
for they shall see God

It is wonderful to look to the heavens on a clear, dark night and marvel at the vast array of stars above us. Magnificent though they are, we only see a minute area of the heavens, for our eye is untrained. When astronomers look to the same heavens they see so much more. They are able to identify the planets and their individual moons, they see shooting stars, comets and even galaxies. They understand the distances in light years between them all and how they relate to one another. It is by these same stars that the skilled navigator steers his ship across stormy seas in the darkest night and brings it in to safe harbour. A very similar illustration is true in the world of art. It is possible for those with an untrained eye to peruse the galleries without recognising the significance of the work they are looking at, unlike trained experts who instantly recognise and fully appreciate the work of the great Masters. The point is this; we see only what we train ourselves to see. We see only what we desire and long to see.

"What God requires of us is this to seek justice, to love kindness and to walk humbly with our God."

Micah 6: 8

The wonderful promise of God is that all who seek Him shall find Him. We have a choice in where to focus our thoughts and with what to do with our time, our energy and our resources. It is so easy to fall into the bad habit of pursuing things that are fleeting and temporary. God longs for us to strive for knowledge of the things of life that are of real and lasting value and which never pass away. God values justice, He calls us to be seekers of justice, not only for ourselves but for those who are unable to speak up for themselves; the disabled, the very young, the elderly, those falsely accused, those confused in mind. They matter! He calls us to "love kindness" and we do this through small acts of love. Lastly God calls us to "walk humbly with Him." We often make the mistake of thinking that we are not good enough, or we feel that we have little to offer Him, we question what talents or gifts we have to give to Him. We've got it wrong when this is our train of thought. God calls us to come to Him with nothing. When we have nothing to give, when we are empty of self, it is then that He fills us with His power.

"Those who are empty, those in want, come to me."

Isaiah 55

There is a story of a man who was passionate about the Japanese philosophy of Zen, he realised his life's dream when he went to Japan to consult a great Zen Master. When he got there he was so excited, he chatted on and on and on to the Master about his knowledge and experiences of Zen. The old Zen Master began to pour him a cup of tea, and when the cup was full to the brim he kept pouring. The man cried out, stop, enough, no more will go in. The Zen Master said to him, "this is you, you have come to me to listen and to learn, but you are so full up already. You have already formed your opinions, you have a static view of things. Why have you come to me? You are so full up already, anything I can teach you would not be taken in for there is no room in your mind for you to receive from me."

Come to God just as you are. Ask Him to fill You, He will! Seek Him, seek justice, pursue goodness and kindness and realise His abundant blessings and inner peace.

Janice Andrews

"Suffering produces perseverance, perseverance,

character; and character, hope."

Romans 5: 3 – 4

Suffering shapes and hones our character

You asked God for strength to achieve things, you experienced weakness and disappointment. It was through this that you learned of His sufficiency and began to trust Him with your life. You wanted riches to enjoy life, you experienced poverty. This gave you a greater awareness of the needs of others and you grew in compassion and self- giving. You wanted to be popular and to have lots of friends, you experienced hurt and loneliness. This taught you about the One who never leaves you, the One in whom you can always trust and through your loneliness you learned to be a better friend to others. You asked that you escape trouble in your life but you experienced many troubles. This honed and shaped your character and built you up in understanding. You learned so much through it all and you are much wiser than if you had not had to endure such tough times. At the time when God did not answer your prayers, it was confusing and you may have asked God "Do You not care? Where are You?"

"Truly God has listened

to the voice of my prayer."

Psalm 66: 19

Surely if God truly loved you He would raise you out of these grave difficulties? The common thread running through all of these questions is "self", we are at the centre of everything. We long for God to yield to our desires, but God hopes that we will trust Him and be willing to yield to **His** perfect will. Imagine a boat sailing into the harbour, a rope is thrown around a bollard on the harbour wall and the rope is pulled. The harbour is not pulled towards the boat! It is through the strength of the harbour that the boat is pulled against it to safety. Christ is your safe harbour, He always hears your prayers. Christ will never abandon you. If He doesn't answer your prayers as you had hoped, keep trusting Him, you may be asking for a change in your circumstances, but what God may be doing is changing your character. Our trials build us up in knowledge and understanding, these are greater treasures than silver or gold, and add substance to our character. It is often only when we look through the rear-view mirror of our lives that we clearly see that our Master's hand has never left us.

"O Love that will not let me go, I rest my weary soul in thee, I give thee back the life I owe, that in thine ocean depths its flow may richer, fuller be."

George Matheson

The Love that never lets us go

Love is so precious and yet so very fragile. There are many ways to lose the people we love, not only through bereavement, although surely this is the most agonising? Glasgow man, George Matheson had his heart broken on more than one occasion. George was extremely bright and embarking on a Theology degree at Glasgow University when he realised that he was losing his sight, studying therefore would be very difficult. In order to help him, his sister, to whom he was very close, also studied Latin, Greek and Hebrew, this was a tremendous support to George. Life was good and the icing on the cake was that George was in love. He'd met a young girl whom he loved deeply and he wished to spend the rest of his life with her. However, when the gravity of his eye condition became fully known, his girlfriend broke off the relationship, feeling unable to cope with George's inevitable blindness. George was devastated. His sister continued to support him and because of her commitment to him, George was able to live a full and fruitful life in Ministry.

Rev Dr George Matheson is buried in Glasgow's
Necropolis.   Through pain and heartbreak, George
discovered the greatest love of all.

However, in time the inevitable happened. His sister met a young man and fell head over heels in love. They began to plan their wedding day. Very soon she too would leave George to make a new life with her husband. George had lost his sight, he'd lost the woman he loved, and he'd lost all hope of having a family of his own, and now it was inevitable that he would have to cope without his beloved sister. On the eve of his sister's wedding, George was reflecting on all that he had lost, when suddenly he became overwhelmed with the realisation of the depth of God's love for him. In these moments George knew that he had a love deeper than any human love, and that it was a love that would never let him go. Deeply moved, George picked up a pen and wrote the words of the beautiful hymn "O love that wilt not let me go". In his moments of deepest despair, he penned the most beautiful words in less than five minutes. It is often when we are heartbroken and acutely aware of the gravity of our loss that the never- ending love of God is brought into the sharpest focus and we realise this the one love that we can never lose.

"Never will I leave you, never will I forsake you."

Hebrews 13: 5

In our troubles God calls us
to be mindful of who He is

Job was desperately seeking answers to his suffering. He had endured the loss of his health, his possessions, and most crushing was the loss of his children. He called out to God with the question many ask "Why?" Why had God abandoned Him? In despair he cried, "I go to the east but You are not there, I go to the west but cannot find You, when You are at work in the north I do not see You, and when I turn south, I cannot glimpse You." Job 23: 9 Job wanted to know where God was in the midst of all his heartbreak and trouble. We wait with baited breath to hear God's reply, for surely this is the one question that no-one can answer, "why do we suffer and where is God in the midst of it all?" God responded in the same way that Jesus often did when He was questioned. Instead of giving straight answers, Jesus often asked a very different question. This was an effective way of leading people to find enlightenment and truth for themselves. In response to Job's plea, God asks him a series of questions. "Where were you when I laid the earth's foundations and marked off its

Janice Andrews

"God views the ends of the earth and sees
everything under the heavens."

Job 28: 24

dimensions? Who was it who laid the first corner stone while the morning stars sang together and the angels shouted for joy? When the sea burst forth from its womb, who commanded it not to cross the boundaries it had been given? Who gives orders to the morning, shows the dawn her place and knows the origin of light?" Job 38

In gently leading Job to consider all these wonders, God gave him greater depth of understanding of His Sovereignty over all life. His are the hands that threw the stars into space, the hands that pull out the heavens at night as if they were a tent, these are the hands that hold us. Despite our troubles and our grief, we are in safe hands, God calls us to believe in what cannot be seen and to trust Him. What God did with Job was to shift the focus of his thinking leading him to rest in His omnipotence. Job was still sad, but he was no longer in turmoil. He trusted in God's Sovereignty, he was able to turn to life and embrace it with renewed strength and inner peace in the one whose hands would never let him go.

"My grace is sufficient for you, for my power is made perfect in weakness."

Corinthians 12: 9

Beauty from brokenness

Two little pots were used to carry water from the river to the house each day. The owner carried them on a pole strapped across his shoulders. One pot was strong and intact and by the time the man reached the house it still had its full supply of water. The other pot was fragile, it had been broken and patched up and some of the water seeped through the cracks. One day the man noticed that the little pot was looking pretty forlorn and he asked it what was wrong. "Well I don't feel very good about myself," said the pot. "I don't do such a great job for you, the other pot gives you much more water than I do." The man picked the pot up and went for a stroll around the garden. On one side of the pathway from the river to the house there was the most beautiful row of flowers. The colours and scents were lovely, they gave the man the greatest pleasure. "What do you think of my beautiful garden?" The man asked the pot. "It is so lovely and must give pleasure to all who visit," the pot replied. The man smiled and said, "do you realise that you are responsible for this loveliness?

"God delights in those who trust Him and who put
their hope in His unfailing love."

Psalm 147: 11

I noticed the water seeping from your cracks and I decided to plant flowers all along your water trail. Each day as we walk back to the house, it is you who refreshes the flowers, it is you who is responsible for all this beauty."

We are just like that little pot. When we have been broken by life we feel fragile and perhaps a little inadequate. God in His perfect wisdom uses our brokenness. He shines His light through all the little cracks in the fabric of our being, bringing a harvest of loveliness. Do not dwell on your flaws or imperfections. Thank God for them, God will use them, it is through your brokenness that you have learned so much. May God fill you with His light. May His light and His love shine through the cracks and flaws of your life that you may be a blessing to others. In His eyes you are perfect. His most precious possession. The apple of His eye. May His love surround you this day and always, rest in the one who brings beauty from brokenness.

"You are the salt of the earth."

Matthew 5: 13

Salt of the earth

It is a great compliment to be referred to as "the salt of the earth", a description of a person who is kind, trustworthy, and truthful, someone who contributes to the life of their community. Salt has many purposes, in the days before fridges and freezers it was rubbed into meat, acting as a preservative and preventing decay. Salt prevents infection and promotes health and cleansing, it purifies, acts as a barrier to infection and brings out flavouring. God is calling us to be the salt of the world, to make a positive contribution to society and act as a barrier to anything that could spoil or contaminate. On a camping holiday a family were having terrible trouble with an infestation of slugs. Every morning they woke to find their tent and everything in it covered in them. They bought a large container of salt and poured it out in a circle around their tent. This acted as a barrier which the slugs never crossed. When we live up to the description "salt of the earth" we too act as a barrier. When gossip, lies, hurtful comments or malice reach our ears it should go no further.

"The light shines in the darkness, and the darkness has not overcome it."

John 1: 5

Light of the world

The smallest candle penetrates the darkest room with light, yet no amount of darkness shall ever overcome the smallest light. The darkness of addiction, hatred, jealousy and abuse, bring grief and brokenness to family life. People are desperate for the things of light; truth, love and peace. Jesus is their source, and He calls us to go into dark situations as bearers of His light that we may show the broken, the lonely and the sad that there is another way of being. There is a love that will never fail them, a friend who will be a true confidante, there is one who cares about justice and truth. The work of Oxfam, Unicef, Tear Fund, Christian Aid, Alcoholics Anonymous and the Hospice movement are only a few of so many charities that do this so well. Where there is poverty, hunger, fear, distress, hopelessness and sickness you will find the light of Christ shining in the greatest darkness. Pursue Christ, ask Him to fill you with His light and go out into the world and shine for Him that others may be guided to the source of light and love.

"I do not understand what I do.   For what I want to do, I do not do, but what I hate, I do."

Romans 7: 15

Our inner battle

Followers of Christ have dual citizenship. We live in the world, but we strive to follow the ways of God. This often creates tension within us, for God's ways and the ways of the world are seldom in alignment. In the world we are faced with lies, suspicion, violence, foolishness and unfaithfulness and we are often disappointed by people or we are the ones who have disappointed others. In the Lord's prayer we ask for the will of God to be done on this earth. The will of God is truth, love, goodness, wisdom, peace, faithfulness, kindness, gentleness. If the Kingdom of God was established on this earth we would all realise the peace that we so desire. All of us contribute to the chaos in the world, none of us are perfect, we all struggle with sin. We often regret the things we've said or attitudes that we're not proud of. The Apostle Paul struggled with sin. He was cross with himself when he did the things that he knew were wrong, and when he failed to do the things that he knew he should. We hope by the grace of God to uphold all that He is, but we are flawed individuals living in a

"Trust in God and do good."

Psalm 37: 3

flawed society and inevitably we at times fail. An Old Cherokee Indian who was teaching his little grandson about life explained this as an internal battle that goes on within us all. He said, "My child, the battle is between two wolves that are inside us all. One is evil, it is angry, and envious, it is jealous, greedy and resentful, it tells lies and has a big ego. The other is good. It is peaceful and kind, generous and compassionate, always truthful and faithful." The boy thought for a minute and then asked his grandfather, "which wolf wins the battle?" The old Cherokee replied, "the one that wins the battle is the one that you feed." When we feed anger and resentment it will grow and fester. When we feed forgiveness and love it will grow and heal. May God keep you hungry for Him. He will build you up in all that is good and true. Seek God, you will find Him in prayer, He is always listening. You will find Him in scripture, His is the living word. You will find Him in love, for His very nature is love. Whatever you face in life, **in His strength,** you will win the battle!

Janice Andrews

"I will be merciful, their sins and iniquities, I will remember no more."

Hebrews 8: 12

When God forgives He forgets

We have all made mistakes in life, and all too often regrets invade our thinking and we are haunted by guilt, this is so damaging. God has forgiven us, but to be free, we must accept His forgiveness or we are in danger of being paralysed by the past. Look at the Apostle Paul, before he discovered the truth about Jesus, he was full of anger, filled with rage and on a mission for revenge. He hated Christ with a passion and in equal measure he hated His followers. In his eyes, followers of Jesus were traitors to Judaism. When he set off on the road to Damascus it was with murder on his mind. Knowing that this was his background, it is incredibly difficult to conceive why, of all men, God chose Paul, a man who had persecuted so many believers in Jesus, to be the man who would go on to be the greatest pioneer of the Christian faith. God opened Paul's eyes to the truth of who Christ is and brought about an incredible transformation in his understanding. Paul was still passionate, but his passion was no longer driven by hate but instead by love. He could do nothing to

"One thing I do, forgetting what is behind and straining towards what is ahead, I press on towards the goal to win the prize for which God has called me heavenwards in Christ Jesus."

Philippians 3: 13 – 14

change his violent past but he could look to the future with hope and live a very different life. In his letter to his friends in Corinth Paul says this, "I am what I am by the grace of God. I am the last man who deserves to be called an Apostle because I persecuted the Church, but God has shown me His immense grace and I have responded to this grace by pouring all that I am into His work." Cor 15: 10. How different the course of the history of the Christian faith and the early Church would be if Paul had chosen to wallow in his mistakes and dwell on how he was perceived by others. He would have been paralysed by guilt and so self-conscious about his bad reputation. Very often this is what we do, we are our own worst enemies. We carry guilt and regret around like a burden when it is so unnecessary. Surely if God is gracious enough to forgive us, we should be gracious enough to receive His forgiveness and move on. When God forgives He forgets. Paul is not defined or remembered for his mistakes. He is the greatest evangelist in Christian history and he helped to make this possible in the manner in which

"I will forgive you and
remember your sins no more."

Hebrews 8: 12

he responded to God's grace.

We will achieve more than we could ever imagine
when we fix our eyes upon Christ Jesus the author
and perfecter of our faith.   We must step out boldly,
putting the past behind us, unconcerned about the
opinions of others, believing that we are defined by
the love of God, upheld in the strength of God, and
able to do abundantly more than we could ever
imagine in and through His grace.

"Let your gentleness be known to all."

Philippians 4: 5

God's manifesto for living

Had the Israelites harboured resentment against the Babylonians it would have been understandable. The Babylonians had robbed them of their possessions, their land and their way of being. However, had they nursed resentment, had they been truculent in conforming to the ways of their new community, what would the Israelites have achieved? The outcome would have been negative all round and detrimental to their long-term wellbeing.

It is not possible to live in anger or resentment when we confess to live in Christ. God calls us to let our gentleness be known to all. Even after the greatest hurts, this is possible in His strength. God calls us to choose gentleness, to choose forgiveness, for this is how God responds to us in the abundance of His grace. Live in the light of Who He is.

"The Son is the image of the invisible God."

Colossians 1: 15

The supremacy of Christ

Jesus once turned to Peter asking this question, "Who do people say that I am?" Peter replied that many thought of Him as a great Prophet, similar to Jeremiah and Elijah, others thought that He was John the Baptist. There are many in the world today who think of Jesus in similar terms. Those who are willing to concede that Jesus was an exceptional man. In fact, if you use Google to search for the ten greatest human beings who have ever lived, Jesus is third on the list alongside Mother Theresa, Buddha, and Ghandi. There have been men and women throughout history who have lived exceptionally good lives and who are great examples of goodness, courage, and wisdom, but none can compare to Christ. To think of Jesus merely in terms of being an exceptionally good man is a million miles from the truth. His birth is the defining moment in the history of time there is life BC and there is life AD. Jesus of Nazareth is an historic figure, but He is not locked in the past.

"I can do all things through Christ

who strengthens me."

Philippians 4: 13

He is the living Son of God, veiled from our sight but omnipresent, listening and loving. He calls us now to follow Him, He will lead us in wisdom and truth and draw us to Himself with chords of love. His paths are not always easy, but they are always good, always true and lead to everlasting peace. Jesus Christ is God incarnate. If we fail to grasp who Jesus is, then we will never truly know who we are. We will measure ourselves only within the limitations of our personal strengths, but this is a pale reflection of all that is truly possible. We are the children of the reigning eternal King and we truly can do all things through Christ who strengthens us.

"We live by faith not by sight."

2 Cor: 5: 7

Faith is a journey

Faith is a journey and it is important that we are equipped for our journey with the right attitude of heart and mind. We have one leader, and that is Christ, ours is the great privilege to serve Him. Jesus is calling us on to new situations, new people, new places it is so easy to feel daunted by the challenge, but we will only lack confidence if our focus is on ourselves and our abilities. This was the mistake Moses made. When God called Him to go to Egypt Moses did not want to go he said "Lord, please pardon me, I am not eloquent in speech please send someone else!"

Exodus 3: 10 – 13

Only after assuring Moses that it would be God Himself who would give him the words to say and bring the task to completion, did Moses agree to go. The success of the exodus of Israel from Egypt was never dependent on Moses, he was simply called to the great privilege of being an instrument in the hands

"He who began a good work in you
will carry it on to completion."

Philippians 1: 6

of God. God will never call you to a task without equipping you to complete it, and He will be with you until His work is done. By His grace may He help you to trust Him and pray the following prayer from one of the earliest believers, "Teach me Lord, to serve You as You deserve; to give and not to count the cost; to fight and not to heed my wounds; to toil and not to demand my rest; to labour and not to expect reward, all in the knowledge that I do Your will." We are so very blessed. No matter where our journey takes us in life or what God calls us to do, our service is not in vain. You are never walking towards the darkness of the night, but always toward the brightness of the dawn.

"The Lord bless you and keep you, the Lord make His face to shine upon you and be gracious unto you, the Lord lift up His countenance upon you and give you peace."

Numbers 6: 22 – 6

Our global citizenship

Jesus came to liberate the world, it is His desire that we are as one as He and the Father are one. There is one God, and one family of God spread across the face of this earth. We have a responsibility to care about our fellow humanity and this responsibility also extends to the created order for we are caught in a web of mutuality, decisions taken by one individual affect many others. There is a wideness in God's mercy, He calls us to share this mercy by seeking justice for the oppressed and by speaking out on behalf of those who cannot speak up for themselves.

There is an abundance in the harvest yielded by the earth. This rich bounty of the land compels us to be thankful and to share with the poor, the hungry and the marginalised. How vulnerable will they be, if we fail in our duty of care? May the glaring injustices of this world serve to encourage us and move us to affirm our common humanity and our corporate responsibility for the world as global citizens.

"I have loved you with an everlasting love,

I have drawn you with unfailing kindness"

Jeremiah 31: 3

You are treasured

Many people in the world today are lost, their self-image has become defined by the expectations of society. Clever marketing and advertising campaigns drive home the message that the measure of man is found in what he has, and in what he has achieved and this leaves many feeling less than adequate. People are climbing various ladders to realise success: the career ladder, the social ladder and the housing ladder. The plan is to get to the top and then spend more time with loved ones. However, the top can turn out to be a very lonely place for somewhere on their journey, in their grasping to have it all, many lose their grip on the real and lasting treasures of life.

We are the children of God. God wants us to enjoy the abundance of His blessings, these are the real and lasting treasures of life that never spoil or fade and cannot be lost, for it is a treasure that is kept in God's safe keeping.

Janice Andrews

"Keep me as the apple of Your eye,
hide me in the shadows of Your wing."

Psalm 17: 8

One young man who had experienced living on the streets estranged from his family told of the day when he asked a passer-by for a £1, when the stranger came towards him he was amazed to recognize that it was his Dad.   Unbeknown to him, his Dad had been walking the streets day after day ever since he left home, longing to find his son that he may bring him home.   The lad had asked for a £1, but it was his Father's desire to give him his all.   It is God's desire that none of us are lost, but that we grasp the measure of His love, a love that moved Him to send His Son into the world that we may be redeemed.   Our heavenly Father longs to bring us home that we may receive our very rich inheritance.   His message to us is this:

You are mine. You have always been mine.   If You go from me, I will pursue you, I will draw You back to me with chords of love.

"In the beginning, when God created the universe,

the earth was formless and desolate."

Genesis 1: 1

Science and Faith

God is deeply concerned about every aspect of our lives, in whatever troubles we have to bear, He is in them with us. He knows our every weakness, He understands the greatest longings of our heart. If you consider the deepest love of a Mother and Father for a vulnerable child, this is only a pale reflection of God's immeasurable love for you. Despite this truth, in recent years there has been rapid growth in secularism, humanism, and atheism in the western world. Many have adopted a world view that denies the presence and the power of an omnipotent Creator. One scientific view is that in time all mysteries will be explained by cosmologists and mathematicians, throwing into question the existence of God. This was not the response of the astronauts who in 1968 went on the first manned orbit of the moon. As they approached lunar sunrise they sent this message from Apollo 8 to all the people on the earth.

"To God belongs the highest heavens,

the earth and everything in it."

Deuteronomy 10: 14

"In the beginning God created the heavens and the earth. The earth was formless and empty, darkness was over the surface of the deep, and the Spirit of God was hovering over the waters, and God said let there be light, and there was light."

The astronauts continued to read the story of creation from the book of Genesis. These men had seen planet earth as no other human beings ever had, and they could respond in no other way than to acknowledge that God is our creator. Science reveals new ideas and solves many mysteries about the universe. New Planets and Solar Systems have been discovered, countless secrets of the outer space have been made known to us through scientific methods, but what science doesn't deal with is our inner space. What response does science have to the heartache of the lonely? How does science enter into our brokenness or understand our grief, or address our rejection, our hurt or terrible worries? What comfort

"The Lord is close to the broken hearted."

Psalm 34: 18

can science give to the bereaved with their ocean of tears? These are the concerns of our inner space that only love can tend, or hope to understand. God is love, He enters into our inner space and tends our open wounds, He speaks into our sadness with tenderness and compassion, and in our weakness, He reassures us of His unfailing strength.

The big bang that is dominant in the minds of all those who follow Jesus is not the detonation that inaugurated the universe, but the rolling away of the stone from the tomb of Christ. This is the defining moment in the history of the world. This is the moment which summoned the death of death.

"What is the kingdom of God like?

To what can I compare it?"

Luke 13: 18

God's Kingdom is advancing

The summer months are a time of abundant growth, fields are lush and green, trees are in full bloom, crops are flourishing and gardens are a sensory delight. However, this growth cannot be measured in real time, for example it is not possible to watch the moment by moment unfolding and blossoming of a flower. This growth only becomes visible when there is a break in time. It is only when we leave our garden for a few days and then return that growth is notable. Similarly, with the Kingdom of God, we see the great advancements that have been made with the help of reflection. Let us consider the dramatic changes experienced by our nation in the recent past: A century ago infant mortality was high, poverty was rife, housing was poor and health care and education were only for those who could afford it. Many social ills that our grandparents endured are now alien to the present generation, and in the previous century things were much worse. In 1817 prison reformer Elizabeth Fry discovered a boy aged 9 in an English prison waiting to be hanged for stealing paint valued at

"Everlasting joy will crown their heads, gladness and joy will overtake them, and sorrow and sighing will flee away."

Isaiah 35: 10b

tuppence! Such a thing in present times would be considered unthinkable, there is no doubt that the Kingdom of God is advancing. In nature's terms, think of how the root of a tree can split a concrete pavement in half, or how weeds stubbornly push through tarmacadam! When nature is determined, nothing can stop her growth. Likewise, there is nothing that humankind can do to thwart the purposes and the plans of God. Finally, at the end of nature's growth, there is the harvest. The fruit and the grain are gathered in, the weeds and the tares are cast aside. God speaks to us about the great harvest of believers: "they will see His face and His name will be on their foreheads." Rev 22: 4.

The Kingdom of God leaves no room for pessimism, no room for doubt. Inevitably we are visited by disappointment and grief, regrets and contrition, but we must never despair. We are the children of the King. Christ has come and Christ shall come again. The Kingdom of God is on the move and nothing will stop its advancement!

"Tears may last for a night,

but it is joy that comes in the morning."

Psalm 30: 5

The night is darkest before the dawn

When the things of life that make us feel safe, begin to slip away from us, it feels very frightening, be it health, security, home, or loved ones. In the greatest storms of life God's voice is heard over all the tumult, calling us to be mindful of Who He is, we can trust Him in all things. The one who commands the wind and the waves to be still is our Pilot. He is at the helm of our lives and He will not fail to guide us into safe harbour. The Apostle Paul faced a blizzard of troubles in his life and yet he endured them all. If we tried to visualize what endurance looks like, we would not think of a person sitting calmly with their head bowed low trying to avoid or escape from their troubles. What we would see is a person with their face set like flint, facing their troubles head on. Pressing forward with great perseverance and determination. This is endurance. Paul had the strength to endure, because although his losses were great, his gain was greater still. Paul kept his eye on the crown of righteousness that he knew, by the grace

"God helps me, therefore I have I set my face like
flint, and I know I will not be put to shame."

Isaiah 50: 7

of God, would be his to receive at the end of his life. As this time approached, he said with confidence, "I have fought a good fight, I have finished the race, and I have kept the faith, now there is in store for me the crown of righteousness which the Lord, the righteous Judge, will award to me on that day."

2 Timothy 4: 7 - 8

The power behind creation is the same power that will uphold you today, and tomorrow and every day. When you feel as if you are walking in a thick fog, unable to see the road ahead, put your hand in the hand of God, set your face like flint, and press on.

"Suppose a brother or sister is without clothes and daily food and you say to them, 'go in peace, keep warm and well fed' but you do nothing about their physical needs, what good is this?"

James 2: 15 - 16

Faith in action

God hates hypocrisy. He is not interested in outward appearances, far too often this is false and insincere. It is our inner being that captures God's attention. One of the main reasons the religious leaders of His day hated Christ was that He exposed their hypocrisy. They failed in their duty of care towards the most vulnerable people in society. They were puffed up with pride. They did things to be seen and admired, enjoying the praises of others and taking their places at the best seats at banqueting tables, but it was what they failed to do that angered Christ. They failed to uphold justice and truth. They lacked compassion, putting unnecessary burdens on those who could least bear them and they turned a blind eye to the plight of orphans and widows. God calls us to love one another. The world is crying out for the needs of the most vulnerable to be met. We cannot help everyone, but we can help someone and when we do, Jesus says that we do it for Him. This is His teaching from Matthew's Gospel:

"People look at the outward appearance, but the
Lord looks at the heart."

1 Samuel 16: 7

"I was hungry and you gave me something to eat,

I was thirsty and you gave me something to drink,

I was a stranger and you invited me in,

I needed clothes and you clothed me,

I was sick and you looked after me,

I was in prison and you came to visit me."

Then the righteous will ask, "Lord, when did we see you hungry and feed you, or thirsty and give you something to drink? When did we see you a stranger and invite you in, or needing clothes and clothe you? When did we see you sick or in prison and go to visit you." The King will reply, "Truly I tell you, whatever you did for one of the least of these brothers and sisters of mine, you did for me."

Matthew 25: 35 - 40

"For God so loved the world that he gave his one and only Son, that whoever believes in him shall not perish but have eternal life."

John 3: 16

The Sovereign power of God

In recent years new words and phrases have been added to our everyday vocabulary, for example, Boko Haram, Isis, and Al Qaeda. These phrases may be new, but throughout history there have always been troubled events perpetuated by rogues who are motivated by hatred, a lust for power, or warped ideologies, this is nothing new. God is sovereign over them all! If we need evidence of this we need look no further than the circumstances that led to the cross. Pontius Pilate was a man of wealth, privilege and power but he was sadly lacking in truth, integrity and justice, he exposed himself to be a man who was impoverished in character and defined by brutality and lies. He knowingly condemned an innocent man to death, this was preferable to being humiliated by the criticism and condescension of religious leaders. These were the same religious leaders who presented false evidence against Jesus. They were hypocrites, they looked like holy men of God on the outside, but God sees the heart, and inwardly they were sadly lacking. They turned a blind eye to the needs of orphans and widows and put unnecessary burdens on

"Death where is your victory?

Where is your sting?"

1 Cor 15: 55

the poor. Then there were those in the crowds who didn't even know their own minds, in their ignorance they became caught up in the fray, baying for the blood of Christ in a frenzy of hatred. All of this, the brutality, the lies, the violence and the injustice were visible for all to see. What was invisible was that God was in control. These characters, Pilate, the Priests and the Pharisees and the angry mob, they were nothing but bit part players in the wonderful drama which was unfolding. The darkness of their actions only served to provide the blackest background against which shone the beauty of God's love and the light of His truth. Jesus' life was not taken from Him! He laid it down and He did this for us. He took our sin upon Himself, in doing so He effectively wiped the slate clean, leaving no debt for us to pay, our sins are paid for in full. Through the horror of the cross, what was unfolding was the most beautiful act of self-giving love. Death has no hold over us, no victory, no sting. It is life that is ours, abundant life, in the very presence of the One Who laid down His life for us.

"Who is this man?" they asked each other.

"Even the wind and waves obey Him!"

Matthew 4: 41

Who is this man?

The Disciples spent every waking moment with Christ they knew Him intimately, but there were moments when they wondered if they knew Him at all, moments when He took their collective breath away, moving them to turn to one another and ask, "who is this man?" Moments when He gave them a revelation of His power, His sovereignty over sickness, over death, over the wind and the waves and the great storms of life, there are always new depths of knowledge to be plunged in regards to Who Christ is. Jesus turned to Peter asking this same question, "who do people say that I am?" Peter replied, well some say that you are a Prophet, others think that you are John the Baptist. "What about you Peter?" asked Jesus, "Who do you say that I am?" Peter replied "You are the Messiah, the Son of God."

How might you answer this same question? "Who do you think that I am?" Your response is important, for you will live accordingly. Christ wants to be

"You are the Messiah, the Son of the living God."

Matthew 16: 16

central in our lives, to be at the core of our being.

However, surrendering all that we are to Him can seem like quite a radical step to take, there is no doubt that it will bring changes to our familiar way of being, but nothing we may lose can compare to what we will gain.   This was Paul's experience.   Paul had been so proud of his credentials as a highly intelligent, well-educated Jewish man, a descendant of the tribe of Benjamin, a man who upheld Jewish law to the letter, scrupulous in his adherence, but everything that had defined him as a fine upstanding educated, holy man of God now paled into insignificance when compared with his new life in Christ.   We have but a brief moment in time to make a difference for Christ in our world   Embrace it!   Christ is asking us to contemplate this morning on Who He is and what this means to our lives.

May you respond with,
"You are the Messiah, the Son of God
come and reign in my life
and for the future take me."

"It was my hand that laid the foundations of the earth, my right hand that spread out the heavens.

Isaiah 48: 13

Working Gloves

One Sunday in Church the Minister told the children a story about going to B & Q to buy a pair of "working gloves". He brought them home and sat them out in his shed saying, "Get to work." A few hours later he popped into the shed to see how things were going, nothing had happened, the gloves hadn't done any work. So, he brought them out of the shed and put them in the garden and said to them, "Come on working gloves, get to work." A few hours later he walked around his garden but again, no work had been done. "Some working gloves these are," he thought to himself. That night he brought them into the house and before he went to bed he said to them, "Working gloves, now get to work, I hope to see a difference in the morning," but when he got up in the morning, still no work had been done. The Minister turned to the children and asked, "Where do you think the man was going wrong?" A wee girl in the front row shot her hand up and replied, "He didn't say please!"

"I am the LORD your God who takes hold of your hand and says to you, do not fear; I will help you."

Isaiah 41: 13

Oh for the innocence and simplicity of a little child. Our hands alone can only do so much but they are transformed into very effective hands that are able to make a real difference in the world when they are placed in the hands of our God.

Clothe your hands in Christ and ask Him to guide you to where there is need, that you may tend others with His gentleness, His goodness and His love. And remember to say please and thank you to the One who equips you for every task.

"God's dream is that you and I and all of us will realise that we are family, we are made for goodness, togetherness and compassion."

Desmond Tutu

A message from the author

May these short reflections encourage you

May you know how precious you are

You are unique

You are God's most treasured possession

You are deeply loved

He is the light that goes before you

Follow His light

Listen to Him

He is perfect wisdom,

Perfect truth

He draws you to Him gently with chords of love

Do not resist Him

Enter ever deeper into His abundant love

Ask Him to use you as His instrument

He will call you to the work of His Kingdom

"Love to all who read this little book"

Janice

"The hunger for love is much more difficult to
remove than the hunger for bread."

Mother Theresa

About the author

Janice is devoted to the Ministry of Musselburgh Congregational Church, she was called to this Ministry on completion of a BA degree in Theology, completing her studies at the International Christian College in Glasgow in 2012. Writing is a simple but effective way of taking the beauty of God's living word beyond Church walls. Janice hopes that readers are encouraged and uplifted, and attracted, like moths to a flame, to the light of Christ.

She is devoted to her children, her grandchildren and especially to her Mum who still lives in Janice's home town of Cumnock, Ayrshire. She visits as often as possible and loves to spend time in the stunning gardens of Dumfries House with her little dog Pippa.

"Then I heard the voice of the Lord saying
Who should I send?   Who will go for Us?"
I said, "Here I am, send me."

Isaiah 6: 8

Mission of writing

Janice published her first book in October 2017. "It's all about Jesus" tells the story of the incarnation of Christ in simple but comprehensive narrative. Copies were sold throughout Europe with all profits being used to provide bricks needed to build a small Sunday School and towards a new Church build. Profits are channelled through Janice's mission partner Liz Gilchrist, a fellow past International Christian College student who hails from Livingston. Liz is a member of King's Church West Lothian in Livingston, a volunteer at Liberton Kirk café and a close friend of Livingston United Parish Church. Liz's mission supports business enterprise in the impoverished villages of Laos, including fish, pig and mushroom farms and sewing projects. The outreach group of Musselburgh Congregational contribute in many different ways to this work. The skills that the young people learn provide them with the means to support themselves, making them less vulnerable to people traffickers.

In memory of Rachel

"May your daughters be like graceful pillars."

Psalm 144: 12

A mission worker in Laos told Liz of a wee girl aged 8 who had been sold to traffickers. The wee girl's Dad had died, and her Mum had no means of holding her family together. The child was traced and was returned to her family after an inflated price of around £25 was paid for her. This child now has hope for her future, her Mum has employment and is able to provide for her children, the story of this one family is an excellent example of how self-empowerment makes these little children less vulnerable. This ministry began with Liz's daughter Rachel to whom this book is dedicated. Rachel was supported throughout her time in Laos by Dedridge Baptist church in Livingston. Thank you to all, and thanks be to God for all that He is doing.

"I AM WHO I AM"

"This is my name from generation to generation."

Exodus 3: 14 - 15

In memory of Rachel

"Very truly I tell you, unless a kernel of wheat falls to the ground and dies, it remains only a single seed, but if it dies, it produces many seeds."

John 12: 24

It is through the work, the love and the Ministry of Rachel Elizabeth Gilchrist that this little book has emerged. May God richly bless Rachel's Mum Liz, my dear friend, a lady who is so rich in faith and obedient in service. In His perfect wisdom God is bringing beauty through brokenness to the little children of Laos.

Printed in Great Britain
by Amazon